NOTEBOOK

FOR THERAPISTS & COUNSELLORS

FOR SESSION NOTES, SUPERVISION THEMES AND MORE

This notebook is ideal to keep all your client notes in one place, as well as jot down themes to take to supervision, client resources needed for the next session, and your thoughts on theories to research raised by material in the session.

Use the index at the front to list each client's ID and the page numbers their notes are on. If, for example, your client has been allotted six sessions, allocate six consecutive double-page spreads to them and jot down the page numbers at the front.

The notebook contains:

- A two-page index at the front to fill in with each client's ID and the page numbers relating to them.
- 60 double-page spreads. The left-hand page is for client session notes; the right-hand one for your notes on resources for the client for next session; themes to take to supervision; theories/ideas for your own learning; and further thoughts.
- This is followed by 50 lined pages for extra notes.

Client ID and
other information

Page number

1.

Date:_____

Client ID:_____

Session notes

Resources for client for next session;

Themes for supervision;

Theories/ideas for my own learning;

Further thoughts

3.

Date:_____

Client ID:_____

Session notes

Resources for client for next session;

Themes for supervision;

Theories/ideas for my own learning;

Further thoughts

5.

Date:_____

Client ID:_____

Session notes

Resources for client for next session;

Themes for supervision;

Theories/ideas for my own learning;

Further thoughts

7.

Date:_____

Client ID:_____

Session notes

Resources for client for next session;

Themes for supervision;

Theories/ideas for my own learning;

Further thoughts

9.

Date:_____

Client ID:_____

Session notes

Resources for client for next session;

Themes for supervision;

Theories/ideas for my own learning;

Further thoughts

11.

Date:_____

Client ID:_____

Session notes

Resources for client for next session;

Themes for supervision;

Theories/ideas for my own learning;

Further thoughts

13.

Date:_____

Client ID:_____

Session notes

Resources for client for next session;

Themes for supervision;

Theories/ideas for my own learning;

Further thoughts

15.

Date:_____

Client ID:_____

Session notes

Resources for client for next session;

Themes for supervision;

Theories/ideas for my own learning;

Further thoughts

17.

Date:_____

Client ID:_____

Session notes

Resources for client for next session;

Themes for supervision;

Theories/ideas for my own learning;

Further thoughts

19.

Date:_____

Client ID:_____

Session notes

Resources for client for next session;

Themes for supervision;

Theories/ideas for my own learning;

Further thoughts

21.

Date:_____

Client ID:_____

Session notes

Resources for client for next session;

Themes for supervision;

Theories/ideas for my own learning;

Further thoughts

_____

_____

_____

_____

_____

_____

_____

_____

_____

_____

_____

_____

_____

_____

_____

_____

_____

_____

_____

Date:_____

Client ID:_____

Session notes

Resources for client for next session;

Themes for supervision;

Theories/ideas for my own learning;

Further thoughts

25.

Date:_____

Client ID:_____

Session notes

Resources for client for next session;

Themes for supervision;

Theories/ideas for my own learning;

Further thoughts

Date:_____

Client ID:_____

Session notes

Resources for client for next session;

Themes for supervision;

Theories/ideas for my own learning;

Further thoughts

29.

Date:_____

Client ID:_____

Session notes

Resources for client for next session;

Themes for supervision;

Theories/ideas for my own learning;

Further thoughts

31.

Date:_____

Client ID:_____

Session notes

Resources for client for next session;

Themes for supervision;

Theories/ideas for my own learning;

Further thoughts

33.

Date:_____

Client ID:_____

Session notes

Resources for client for next session;

Themes for supervision;

Theories/ideas for my own learning;

Further thoughts

35.

Date:_____

Client ID:_____

Session notes

Resources for client for next session;

Themes for supervision;

Theories/ideas for my own learning;

Further thoughts

Date:_____

Client ID:_____

Session notes

Resources for client for next session;

Themes for supervision;

Theories/ideas for my own learning;

Further thoughts

Date:_____

Client ID:_____

Session notes

Resources for client for next session;

Themes for supervision;

Theories/ideas for my own learning;

Further thoughts

_____

_____

_____

_____

_____

_____

_____

_____

_____

_____

_____

_____

_____

_____

_____

_____

_____

_____

41.

Date:_____

Client ID:_____

Session notes

Resources for client for next session;

Themes for supervision;

Theories/ideas for my own learning;

Further thoughts

43.

Date:_____

Client ID:_____

Session notes

Resources for client for next session;

Themes for supervision;

Theories/ideas for my own learning;

Further thoughts

_____

_____

_____

_____

_____

_____

_____

_____

_____

_____

_____

_____

_____

_____

_____

_____

_____

_____

_____

_____

45.

Date:_____

Client ID:_____

Session notes

Resources for client for next session;

Themes for supervision;

Theories/ideas for my own learning;

Further thoughts

Date:_____

Client ID:_____

Session notes

Resources for client for next session;

Themes for supervision;

Theories/ideas for my own learning;

Further thoughts

Date:_____

Client ID:_____

Session notes

Resources for client for next session;

Themes for supervision;

Theories/ideas for my own learning;

Further thoughts

51.

Date:_____

Client ID:_____

Session notes

Resources for client for next session;

Themes for supervision;

Theories/ideas for my own learning;

Further thoughts

53.

Date:_____

Client ID:_____

Session notes

Resources for client for next session;

Themes for supervision;

Theories/ideas for my own learning;

Further thoughts

55.

Date:_____

Client ID:_____

Session notes

Resources for client for next session;

Themes for supervision;

Theories/ideas for my own learning;

Further thoughts

Date:_____

Client ID:_____

Session notes

Resources for client for next session;

Themes for supervision;

Theories/ideas for my own learning;

Further thoughts

59.

Date:_____

Client ID:_____

Session notes

Resources for client for next session;

Themes for supervision;

Theories/ideas for my own learning;

Further thoughts

61.

Date:_____

Client ID:_____

Session notes

Resources for client for next session;

Themes for supervision;

Theories/ideas for my own learning;

Further thoughts

63.

Date:_____

Client ID:_____

Session notes

Resources for client for next session;

Themes for supervision;

Theories/ideas for my own learning;

Further thoughts

65.

Date:_____

Client ID:_____

Session notes

Resources for client for next session;

Themes for supervision;

Theories/ideas for my own learning;

Further thoughts

Date:_____

Client ID:_____

Session notes

Resources for client for next session;

Themes for supervision;

Theories/ideas for my own learning;

Further thoughts

69.

Date:_____

Client ID:_____

Session notes

Resources for client for next session;

Themes for supervision;

Theories/ideas for my own learning;

Further thoughts

71.

Date:_____

Client ID:_____

Session notes

Resources for client for next session;

Themes for supervision;

Theories/ideas for my own learning;

Further thoughts

73.

Date:_____

Client ID:_____

Session notes

Resources for client for next session;

Themes for supervision;

Theories/ideas for my own learning;

Further thoughts

75.

Date:_____

Client ID:_____

Session notes

Resources for client for next session;

Themes for supervision;

Theories/ideas for my own learning;

Further thoughts

Date:_____

Client ID:_____

Session notes

Resources for client for next session;

Themes for supervision;

Theories/ideas for my own learning;

Further thoughts

Date:_____

Client ID:_____

Session notes

Resources for client for next session;

Themes for supervision;

Theories/ideas for my own learning;

Further thoughts

81.

Date:_____

Client ID:_____

Session notes

Resources for client for next session;

Themes for supervision;

Theories/ideas for my own learning;

Further thoughts

Date:_____

Client ID:_____

Session notes

Resources for client for next session;

Themes for supervision;

Theories/ideas for my own learning;

Further thoughts

85.

Date:_____

Client ID:_____

Session notes

Resources for client for next session;

Themes for supervision;

Theories/ideas for my own learning;

Further thoughts

Date:_____

Client ID:_____

Session notes

Resources for client for next session;

Themes for supervision;

Theories/ideas for my own learning;

Further thoughts

89.

Date:_____

Client ID:_____

Session notes

Resources for client for next session;

Themes for supervision;

Theories/ideas for my own learning;

Further thoughts

91.

Date:_____

Client ID:_____

Session notes

Resources for client for next session;

Themes for supervision;

Theories/ideas for my own learning;

Further thoughts

Date:_____

Client ID:_____

Session notes

Resources for client for next session;

Themes for supervision;

Theories/ideas for my own learning;

Further thoughts

95.

Date:_____

Client ID:_____

<u>Session notes</u>

Resources for client for next session;

Themes for supervision;

Theories/ideas for my own learning;

Further thoughts

97.

Date:_____

Client ID:_____

Session notes

Resources for client for next session;

·Themes for supervision;

Theories/ideas for my own learning;

Further thoughts

Date:_____

Client ID:_____

Session notes

Resources for client for next session;

Themes for supervision;

Theories/ideas for my own learning;

Further thoughts

101.

Date:_____

Client ID:_____

Session notes

Resources for client for next session;

Themes for supervision;

Theories/ideas for my own learning;

Further thoughts

103.

Date:_____

Client ID:_____

Session notes

Resources for client for next session;

Themes for supervision;

Theories/ideas for my own learning;

Further thoughts

105.

Date:_____

Client ID:_____

Session notes

Resources for client for next session;

Themes for supervision;

Theories/ideas for my own learning;

Further thoughts

107.

Date:_____

Client ID:_____

Session notes

Resources for client for next session;

Themes for supervision;

Theories/ideas for my own learning;

Further thoughts

109.

Date:_____

Client ID:_____

Session notes

Resources for client for next session;

Themes for supervision;

Theories/ideas for my own learning;

Further thoughts

111.

Date:_____

Client ID:_____

Session notes

Resources for client for next session;

Themes for supervision;

Theories/ideas for my own learning;

Further thoughts

113.

Date:_____

Client ID:_____

Session notes

Resources for client for next session;

Themes for supervision;

Theories/ideas for my own learning;

Further thoughts

115.

Date:_____

Client ID:_____

Session notes

Resources for client for next session;

Themes for supervision;

Theories/ideas for my own learning;

Further thoughts

117.

Date:_____

Client ID:_____

Session notes

Resources for client for next session;

Themes for supervision;

Theories/ideas for my own learning;

Further thoughts

119.

Date:_____

Client ID:_____

Session notes

Resources for client for next session;

Themes for supervision;

Theories/ideas for my own learning;

Further thoughts

_____

_____

_____

_____

_____

_____

_____

_____

_____

_____

_____

_____

_____

_____

_____

_____

_____

_____

_____

_____

Notes

Notes

Notes

Notes

Notes

Notes

Notes

Notes

Notes

Notes

Notes

Notes

Notes

Notes

Notes

Notes

Notes

Notes

139.

Notes

Notes

Notes

Notes

Notes

Notes

Notes

Notes

Notes

Notes

Notes

Notes

Notes

Notes

Notes

Notes

155.

Notes

Notes

Notes

Notes

Notes

Notes

161.

Notes

Notes

Notes

Notes

165.

Notes

Notes

Notes

Notes

Notes

Notes

Made in the USA
Coppell, TX
27 April 2021

54586097R00096